Earthquakes

William B. Rice

Earthquakes

Publishing Credits

Associate Editors
James Anderson
Torrey Maloof

Editorial Director
Dona Herweck Rice

Editor-in-Chief
Sharon Coan, M.S.Ed.

Creative Director
Lee Aucoin

Illustration Manager
Timothy J. Bradley

Publisher
Rachelle Cracchiolo, M.S.Ed.

Science Consultant
Scot Oschman, Ph.D.

Teacher Created Materials
5301 Oceanus Drive
Huntington Beach, CA 92649-1030
http://www.tcmpub.com

ISBN 978-1-4333-0309-8

Table of Contents

Always Changing

Nothing ever stays the same. People through time have said that very thing, and it is true. No matter what something is, in time it will change. Things that do not seem to change at all will change. Even Earth itself changes.

If you were sitting in the same spot you are now, ten million years ago, you would see a different world. Not only would everything people have built be gone but the land would also be different. The mountains in the distance might not be there. The rocks on the sides of those mountains might be below ground. Nearby valleys might be below the ocean.

The earth shifts and changes all the time. Much of the change is very slow. But sometimes the changes come fast, even in an instant.

This valley was created over millions of years.

Sloooowwww

It can take a mountain range hundreds of millions of years to form. Most changes to the planet are very slow.

What Makes an Earthquake?

What could possibly happen to make the Earth change fast? One big factor is an **earthquake**. An earthquake is the movement of land caused by plates in the Earth's crust rubbing past, into, or against each other. When this happens, sometimes the plates get stuck. **Pressure** builds. When the plates can't take the pressure anymore, they give way. The pressure must go somewhere. Earthquake!

This crack in the Earth's surface was caused by an earthquake at a fault line.

Earthquakes can have dramatic effects on people and the land.

Thousands of small earthquakes happen every day around the planet. They are so small that no one feels them. Only a few dozen each year can be felt by people on the surface. Of those, a small few are felt by many people and do a great deal of damage. Large earthquakes change the land quickly. The land can crack, shift, rise, or fall. Everything on or near it is affected.

Seismologists

Scientists who study earthquakes are called **seismologists** (size-MOL-uh-jists). Seismologists use machines to sense earthquakes that people can and cannot feel. The machines help seismologists learn about earthquakes and the Earth.

Crusty

Earth's crust is about 40 kilometers (25 miles) thick at the continents. It is about 7 kilometers (4 miles) thick under the oceans.

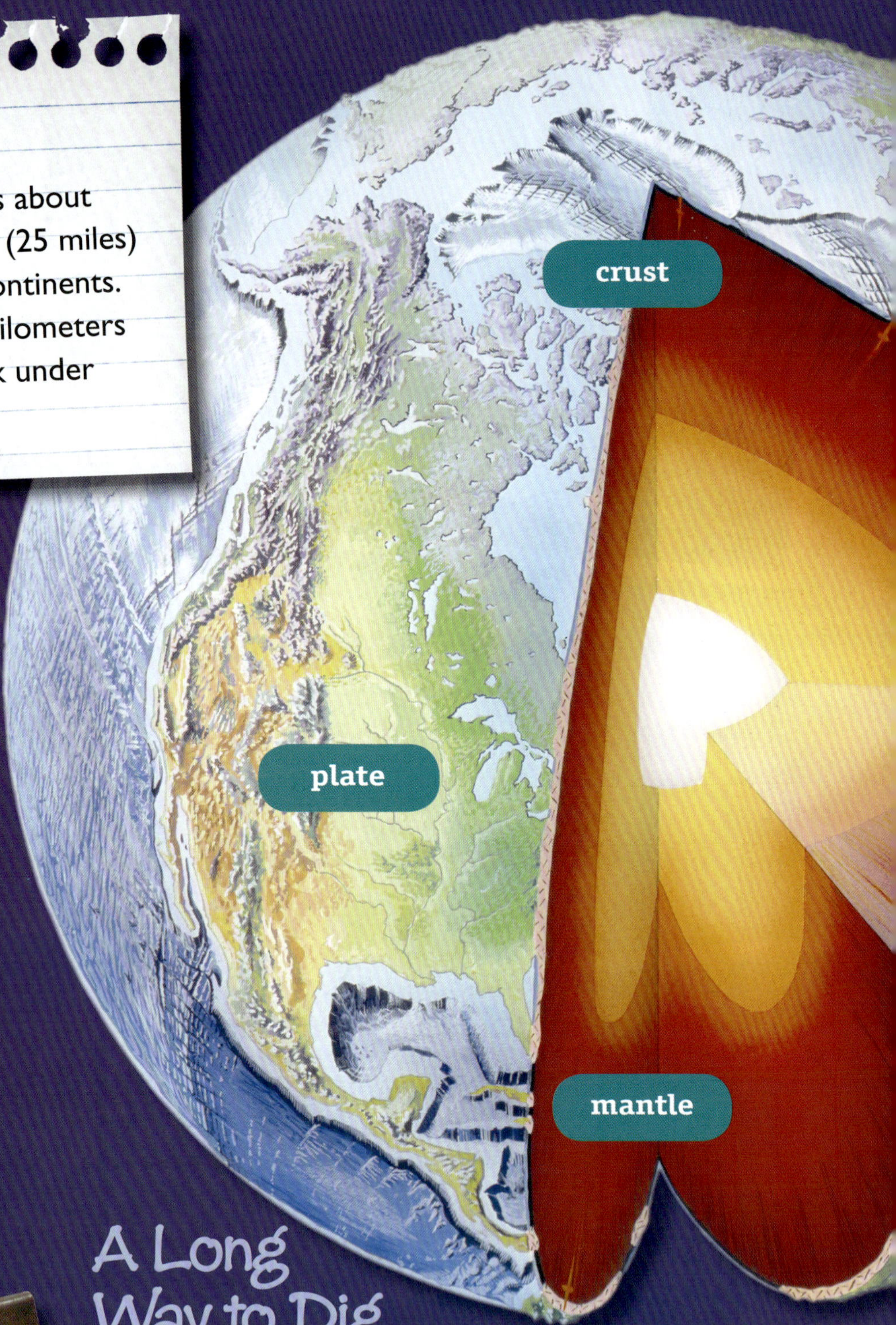

A Long Way to Dig

If you wanted to reach Earth's center, you would have to dig down 6,400 kilometers (4,000 miles).

Plate Movement

Earth's outer layer, the **crust**, is not one solid, smooth piece. It is broken up into many large pieces. Each piece is called a **plate**. The plates are made of Earth materials such as rocks and minerals. Some plates are larger than continents. Some plates are smaller, like a country. Either way, plates are huge.

Earth is made of many layers. The crust is rigid and brittle. It sits on top of the **mantle**, which is more fluid. Earth's plates float on top of the liquid rock beneath them. As the liquid mantle flows, the plates float along as well. As they float, they rub against each other in different ways. No matter which way they meet, earthquakes will happen.

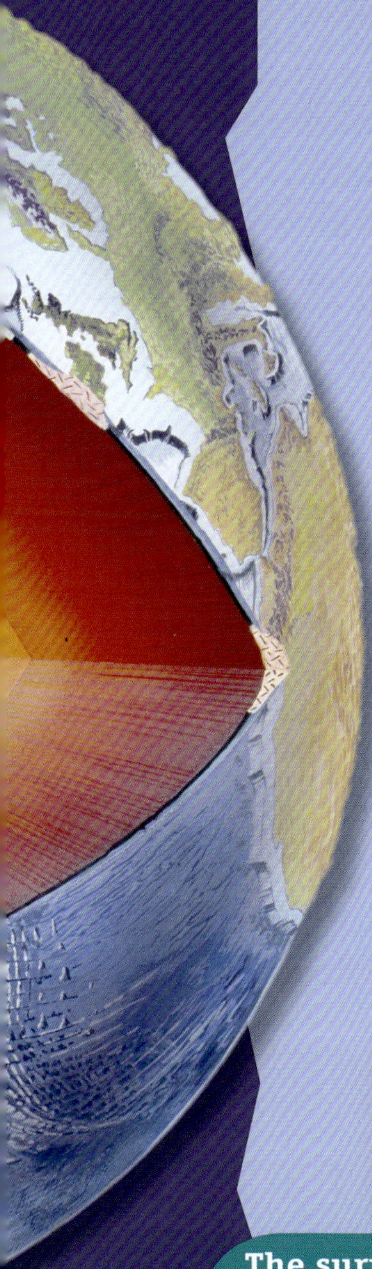

The surface that you see around you is part of Earth's crust.

The place where plates meet is called a **boundary**. There are three main types of boundaries. They are **convergent** (kuhn-VUR-juhnt), **divergent** (di-VUR-juhnt), and **transform**. The difference among them is the way in which the plates move in relation to each other.

A convergent boundary is where two plates move toward each other. When they meet, one of the plates usually moves on top of the other. A divergent boundary is where two plates move away from each other. New crust is made as they move apart. A transform boundary is where two plates slide past each other.

These boundaries have helped to make many features on Earth's surface. These features are things such as mountains, valleys, and islands. New features are being created all the time.

Growing Earth

The Atlantic Ocean is spreading about two centimeters ($\frac{3}{4}$ inch) per year. That is a growth during your lifetime of about the length of an adult's body!

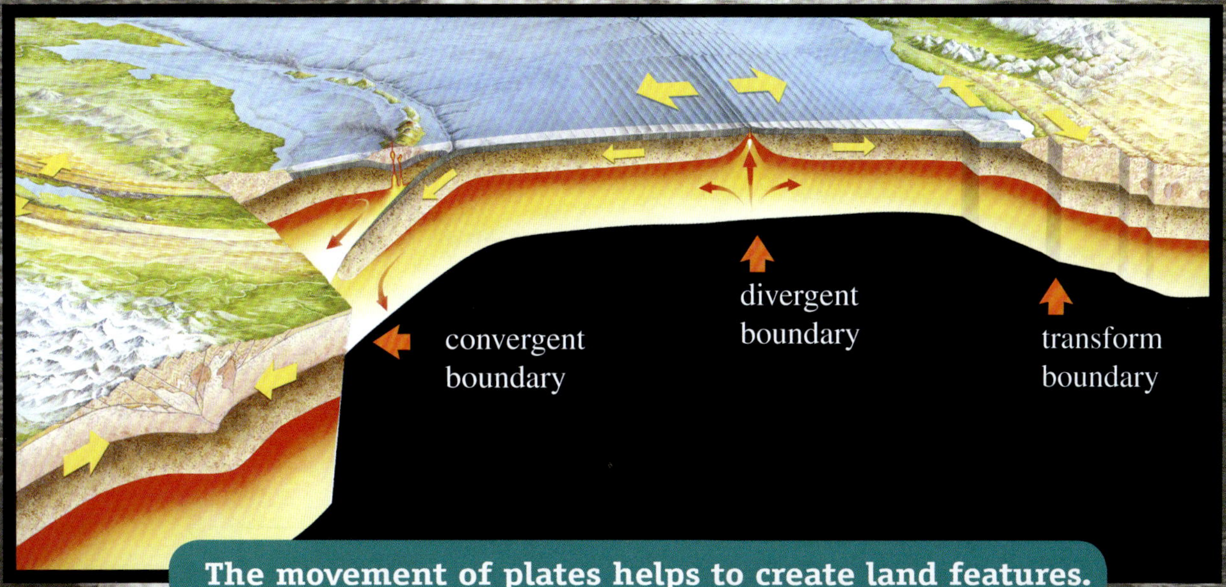

The movement of plates helps to create land features.

Where Do Earthquakes Happen?

Earthquakes can happen anywhere on the planet. But they happen more often in some places than they do in others. They happen mostly at plate boundaries. Pressure builds at plate boundaries and is released as the plates slide past each other.

This map shows common earthquake locations around the world.

Andes Mountains

Sliding Under

In a convergent boundary, when a plate with oceanic crust runs into a plate with continental crust, the plate with oceanic crust will slide under the plate with continental crust.

One place that earthquakes happen a lot is along the west coast of South America. Here, one plate goes over the top of another plate. The plate on top is the South American plate. The plate below is the Nazca (NAHS-kuh) plate. They meet at a convergent boundary. Their boundary has helped to create the Andes Mountains. It has also helped to create one of the biggest lakes in the world. It is called Lake Titicaca (tee-tee-KAH-kuh).

Lake Titicaca

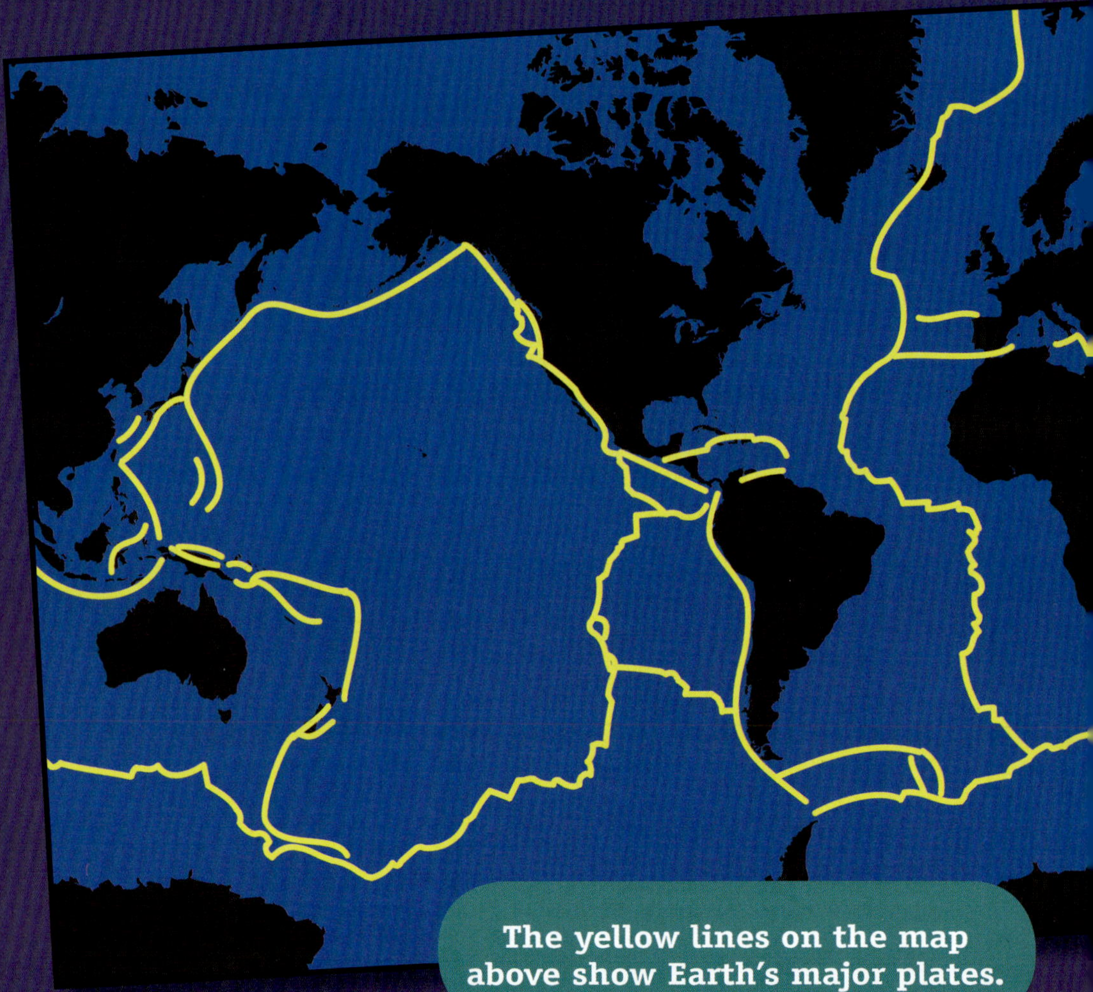

The yellow lines on the map above show Earth's major plates.

young rocks in Iceland

Young Rocks

The rocks that make up Iceland are some of the youngest rocks in the world. The youngest of those rocks can be found at or near the plate boundaries.

a bridge spans divergent plates in Iceland

Another place that has many earthquakes is Iceland. Iceland is a large island in the middle of the Atlantic Ocean. Here, two plates move away from each other. One plate is the Eurasian plate. The other is the North American plate. They meet at a divergent boundary.

The plates move away from each other about two to four centimeters (one to two inches) each year. As they pull apart, new crust is made at the boundary. So much new crust has been made that the land built up above the water and formed Iceland. Iceland keeps growing because of this. Who knows how large Iceland might grow to be in the future?

California also has many earthquakes. There are thousands there each year. Two plates slide past each other in California. One is the North American plate. The other is the Pacific plate. They meet at a transform boundary.

The two plates move past each other at about five centimeters (two inches) per year. That is about how fast your fingernails grow each year.

Mountains and valleys have formed at this boundary. But they are nowhere near as big as the ones formed at convergent boundaries. The plate movement at the boundary also affects bodies of water. Some rivers flow across the boundary. They change their course as the plates move during an earthquake.

This image of the San Andreas fault was taken from an airplane.

Rivers that cross the San Andreas Fault may change their course during and after an earthquake.

San Andreas Fault

The San Andreas Fault in California is a famous transform boundary. It is actually not a single fault line. It is really made of many segments. It is about 1,300 kilometers (800 miles) long.

This image of the San Andreas fault was taken from space.

A Short Trip

Because of plate movement, scientists think that the cities of Los Angeles and San Francisco will be right next to each other in about 15 million years!

What Happens During an Earthquake?

Earthquakes happen no matter the type of boundary. They happen because of **friction** (FRIK-shuhn) and pressure.

Friction is a force. It acts on surfaces to slow things down or stop them from moving. It is like skidding to a stop with your bicycle. Your tire rubbing against the pavement is where friction takes place. Some rubber gets left on the pavement, making a skid mark. The pavement rubbing against the tire is the force that slows the bike down. That force is friction. The bicycle brake has stopped the wheel from turning. But added friction happens between the tire and the pavement.

Friction acts against the direction of motion. In the bike example, friction makes the bike stop. It stops because the bike is moving one way and friction from the pavement pushes against it. If friction acted in the same direction, the bike would just go faster.

When a bike skids to a stop, the skid mark is caused by friction.

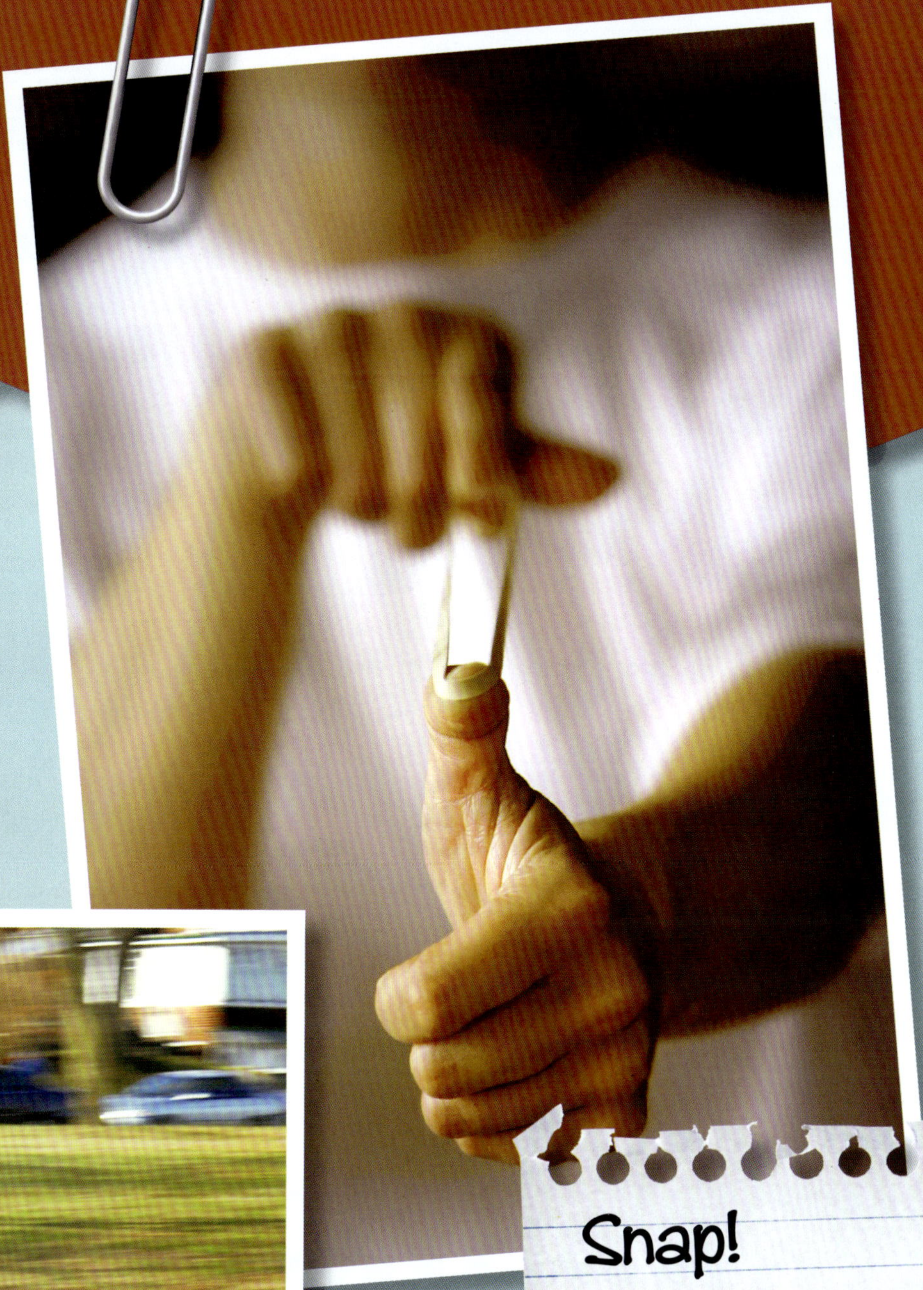

Snap!

Another way to think of an earthquake is like stretching a rubber band. Imagine stretching it more and more until it finally breaks. That is how an earthquake happens. The pressure builds, and then—snap!

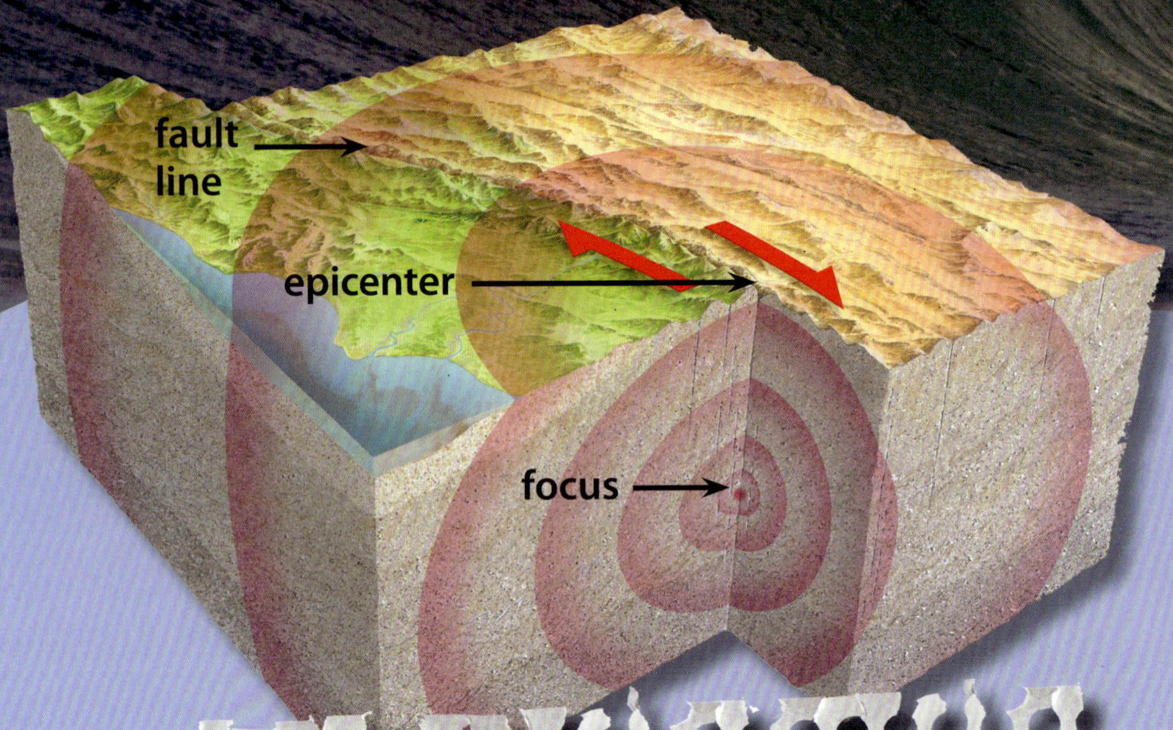

Not a Straight Line

A boundary is not a straight line. It curves and bends. Where it curves and bends along converging or transform plates, pressure builds. It is like trying to push two rough surfaces past each other. It would be hard to make them slide easily and smoothly.

Earthquakes below the ocean floor can cause giant waves to hit land nearby or far away.

At a plate boundary, two plates move in different directions. There is friction between the plates. The friction can stop them from moving. When this happens, pressure builds. The pressure builds up so much that the plates suddenly skid past each other. Then there is an earthquake.

The point deep underground where the Earth's crust actually snaps is called the **focus**. It is the center of the earthquake. The **epicenter** is the place at Earth's surface just above the focus.

The closer you are to the epicenter, the more you will feel the earthquake. Most damage is done near the epicenter. But a large earthquake can be felt very far away. And an epicenter below the ocean can cause giant waves of water to hit the land.

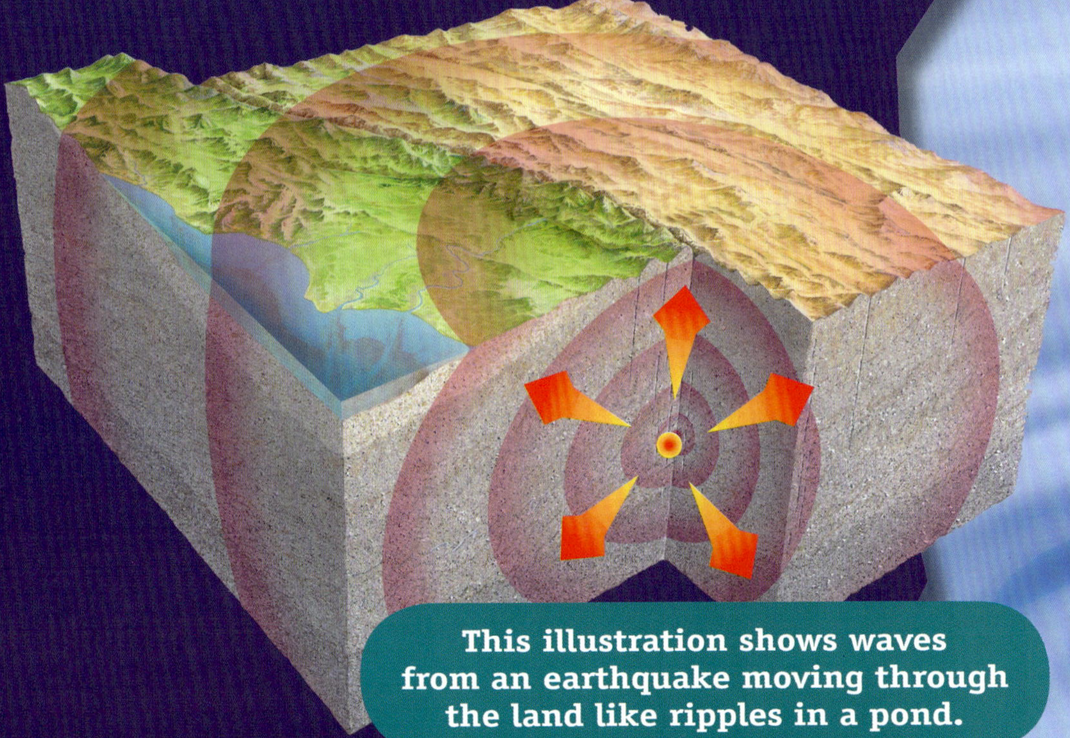

This illustration shows waves from an earthquake moving through the land like ripples in a pond.

When an earthquake happens, pressure is released. The energy moves out from the focus. Think about when a stone is thrown into a pond. Ripples move out from where the stone hit the water. The ripples are little waves. Pressure released from an earthquake is like that. Energy moves out through the Earth like waves in a pond.

The power of the waves depends on the size of the earthquake. When there is a big earthquake, we feel a lot of shaking as the waves reach us. We may not feel the waves of a small earthquake at all. But even if we do not feel them, the waves still happen. Even small earthquakes and small waves affect Earth.

Seiche

Have you ever held a bowl of water and sloshed it back and forth? Water rushes up the sides of the bowl from side to side. Some of the water sloshes out. This is exactly what can happen to a lake during an earthquake. This is called a **seiche** (SAYSH).

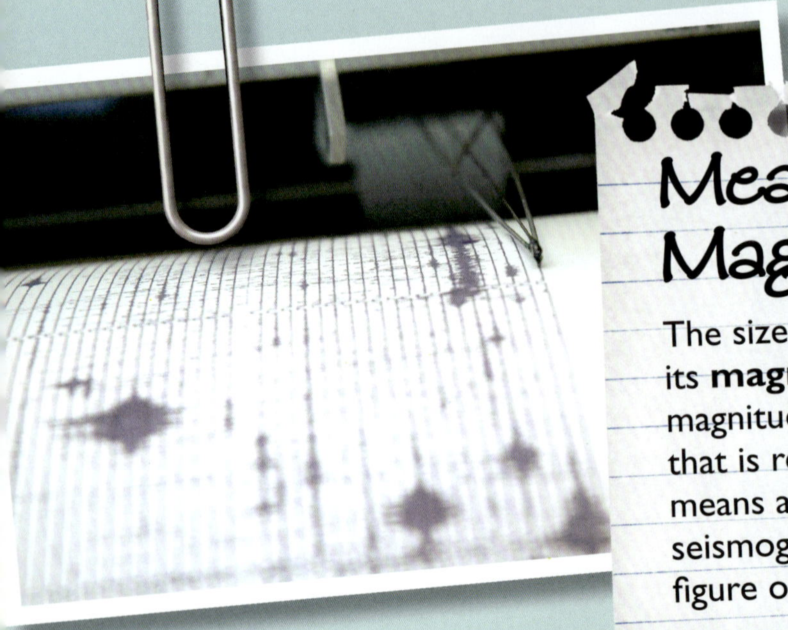

Measuring Magnitude

The size of an earthquake is called its **magnitude** (MAG-ni-tood). The magnitude is the amount of energy that is released. A high magnitude means a big earthquake. Scientists use seismographs like the one on the left to figure out an earthquake's magnitude.

Land shifts during an earthquake. Because it does, things on the land can shift, too.

People can feel some earthquakes. They feel shaking and rolling. Small earthquakes might wake them from a sound sleep. Bigger earthquakes can make things fall off shelves in houses and stores. Walls may be cracked. Large earthquakes may knock down furniture and walls. Giant earthquakes may crumble houses and bridges. Even big buildings may fall!

Sometimes, the effects after an earthquake are worse than the earthquake itself. Earthquakes can cause fires. If pipes that carry gas are broken, the gas can ignite. Water pipes may also break. Then people in houses can't get their water.

Richter Scale

The magnitude of an earthquake has long been measured on the **Richter** (RIK-ter) **Scale**. This chart shows Richter measurements and how often they happen.

Description	Richter Magnitude	Effect	How Often It Occurs
micro	less than 2.0	none	about 8,000 per day
minor	2.0–2.9	none	about 1,000 per day
minor	3.0–3.9	felt, but rarely causes damage	49,000 per year
light	4.0–4.9	shaking of items; usually no damage	6,200 per year
moderate	5.0–5.9	major damage to poorly made buildings; slight damage to well-made buildings	800 per year
strong	6.0–6.9	destructive in areas up to about 160 kilometers (100 miles)	120 per year
major	7.0–7.9	serious damage over larger areas	18 per year
great	8.0–8.9	serious damage in areas several hundred kilometers/miles across	1 per year
great	9.0–9.9	devastating in areas several thousand kilometers/miles across	1 per 20 years
great	10.0+	never recorded	

There is no limit to the amount of destruction an earthquake can cause.

Earthquakes Keep Happening

Earth's plates have always been on the move. Chances are good that they will continue to move in the future. Because of this, earthquakes will keep on happening.

Scientists will always want to study earthquakes to learn more about them and the Earth. They will also want to learn more about making safe and strong buildings, bridges, and houses. If they are strong, people can stay safe.

No one can predict exactly where or when an earthquake will strike. But we do know that every earthquake will change the Earth. Sometimes the changes will be big. Sometimes they will be small. Maybe we won't even be able to see the changes. But whether big or small, every earthquake leaves its mark.

Lab: Pangea Puzzle

The theory of plate motion, also called continental drift, was first suggested not very long ago. Scientists saw that the continents seemed to fit together like a puzzle. Along with other evidence, this made them think that perhaps all the continents had once been part of a large land mass called Pangea.

Today we know a lot about plate movement. Pangea seems quite possible. Do this activity to check it out for yourself.

Materials

- a copy of the continents on the next page
- scissors

Procedure:

1. Make a copy of the continents on the next page. You will probably want to enlarge them.
2. Cut out the continents.
3. Try putting the pieces of the continents together as if they were a puzzle.

Conclusion:

Does Pangea seem likely to you? Do the pieces seem to fit together? Research to learn more about Pangea and continental drift.

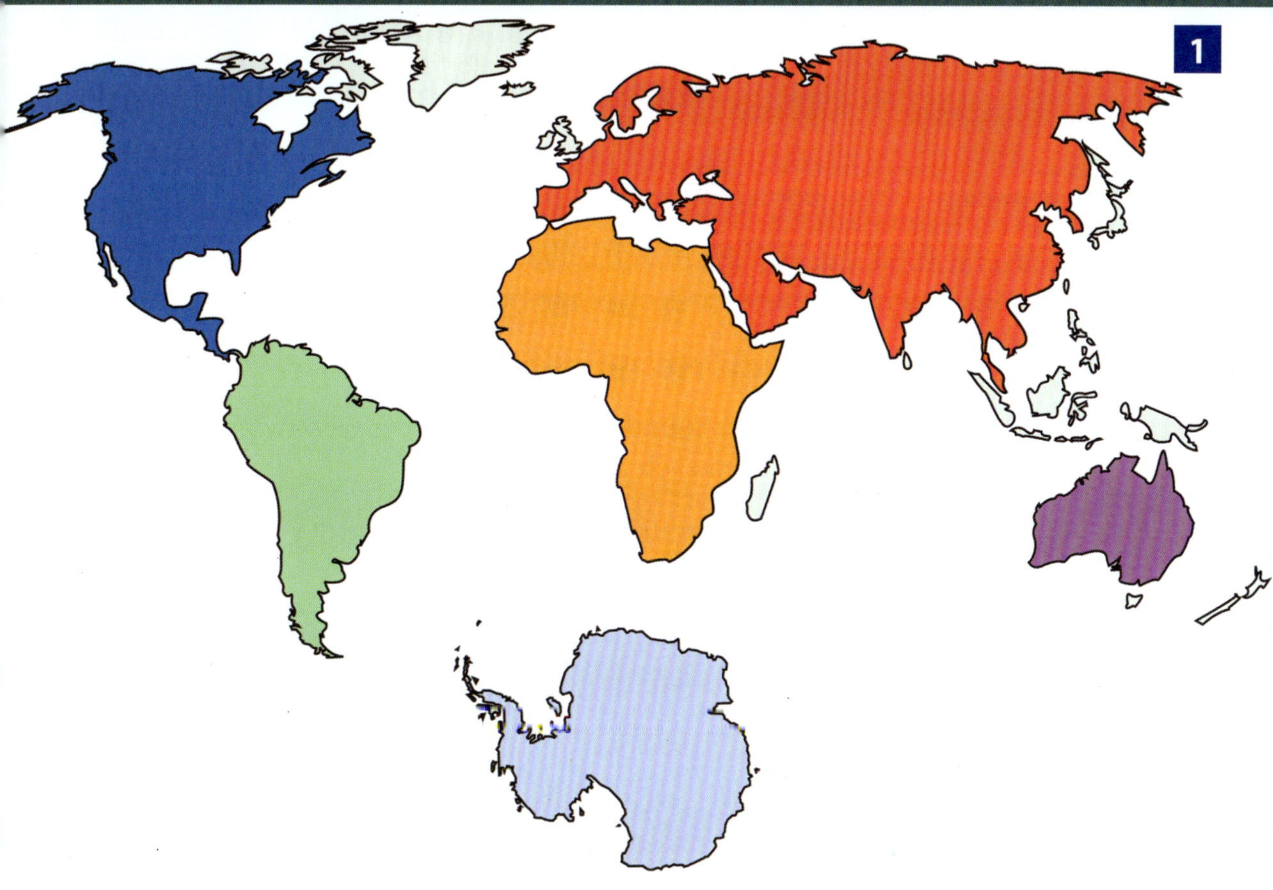
1

2

Glossary

boundary—edge, border, or limit

convergent boundary—the boundary that occurs between two plates that are moving toward each other

crust—the solid, brittle upper layer of Earth

divergent boundary—the boundary that occurs between two plates that are moving away from each other

earthquake—a shaking, vibrating, or upheaval of Earth's surface caused by the movement of plates in the crust

epicenter—the point on the surface of Earth directly above the focus of an earthquake

focus—the center of the earthquake, beneath Earth's surface

friction—a force that acts on surfaces that are in contact with each other and slows them down or stops them from moving

magnitude—size

mantle—the hot, molten, second layer of Earth, just below the crust

plate—a section of Earth's crust

pressure—the exertion of force upon a surface by an object, fluid, or other source in contact with it

Richter Scale—the scale used to measure the strength of earthquakes

seiche—the sudden back-and-forth movement of water in a lake or other body of water, caused by an earthquake

seismologist—scientist who studies earthquakes

transform boundary—the boundary that occurs between two plates that are sliding past each other

Index

Scientists Then and Now

Alfred Wegener
(1880–1930)

Alfred Wegener was an astronomer at first. But one day, the continents caught his interest. He noticed the coastlines. He thought they looked like puzzle pieces. Wegener developed a theory called continental drift. The theory says that the continents were once attached but broke apart and drifted away over time. Wegener's theory led to the study of plate movement, called plate tectonics.

Tanya Atwater
(1944–)

Tanya Atwater is a professor and a scientist. She loves the natural world, and she wants others to love it, too. That is why she teaches. She hopes that she can teach others to respect and care for the planet. Atwater especially studies plate tectonics. Sometimes, she takes a submersible boat all the way to the ocean floor to study sea floor spreading up close!

Image Credits

Cover Kiyoshi Ota/Getty Images; p.1 Kiyoshi Ota/Getty Images; p.4-5 Joseph Gareri/Shutterstock; p.6 Joshua Blake/iStockphoto; p.7(top) USGS; p.7(bottom) David R. Frazier Photolibrary, Inc./Alamy; p.8-9 Gary Hincks/Photo Researchers, Inc.; p.9 cinoby/iStockphoto; p.10-11 Rui Vale de Sousa/Shutterstock; p.11 Gary Hincks/Photo Researchers, Inc.; p.12 Cartesia/LKPalmer; p.13(top) Galyna Andrushko/Shutterstock; p13(bottom) Suzanne Long/Shutterstock; p.14(top) Stephanie Reid; p.14(bottom) Vera Bogaerts/Shutterstock; p.15 Chris73/Wikipedia; p.16-17 USG; p.16 Tom Bean/Corbis; p.17 NASA/JPL; p.18-19 Elena Elisseeva/Shutterstock; p.19 Bradley Mason/iStockphoto; p.20 Gary Hincks/Photo Researchers, Inc.; p.20-21 mollypix/Shutterstock; p.22 Gary Hincks/Photo Researchers, Inc.; p.22-23 Fesus Robert/Shutterstock; p.23 Neil Bromfield/iStockphoto; p.24(top) Furchin/iStockphoto; p.24(bottom) Pacific Press Service/Alamy; p.26(top) Newscom; p.26-27(bottom) USGS; p.26-27(top) USGS; p.29 Tim Bradley; p.32(left) The Granger Collection, New York; p.32(right) Rick Reason.